Let's Decide Together

Practicing Sociocracy with Children

by Hope Wilder

Sociocracy For All
Amherst, MA USA
sociocracyforall.org

Sociocracy For All

20 Pulpit Hill Road, Unit 8

Amherst MA, 01002

United States of America

info@sociocracyforall.org

Published by Sociocracy For All. Sociocracy For All is a project of Institute for Peaceable Communities (IPC), an incorporated 501(c)(3) non-profit organization in Massachusetts, USA.

© Hope Wilder 2021. All words in this volume are available under a Creative Commons Attribute-ShareAlike Non-commercial 4.0 License.

https://creativecommons.org/licenses/by-nc-sa/4.0/

Includes diagrams, illustrations, and references.

ISBN: 978-1-949183-10-8

Cover design © Sociocracy for All 2021

Cover design by Shena Honey L. Pulido

Testimonials

"My kiddo feels so empowered during family meetings now and it takes so much stress out of chores and other day-to-day activities. I'd recommend Let's Decide Together to anyone working with kids."

—Erik Gillespie, parent

"I like that everyone gets to agree instead of most people. I don't know what to say, it's just awesome."

—Kira Gillespie, age 8

"With this book Hope has provided an accessible step-by-step guide for actual implementation of shared power with young people. It's great! I really appreciate the examples shared (along with all the worksheets and templates), facilitative tips, and change-up meeting guide (see Chapter 5). I hope you, like me, will try to dig into this book and bring these techniques to connect and work with youth. Looking forward to deciding together!"

—Will Gowen, Director of Programs at School Around Us Co-Learning Community

"The key to the treasure chest of a new paradigm for the institutions of school and family!"

—Gina Simm, author of *Heart to Heart: 3 Systems for Staying Connected*

"This is such a heart-warming book! It provides practical guidance and inspiration on how to use Sociocracy with children in a fun and light way. You can also have a feeling of how it is to be inside a democratic school and learn from a real experience. I highly recommend it to anyone looking for ways to listen to and collaborate with children and youth!"

—Marianne Osorio, director of *School Circles* film and
founder of Wondering School

Contents

- Introduction 1
  - Why Sociocracy with Children 2
  - What Is Sociocracy 4
  - About This Book 5
  - Common Questions 8
  - What Will You Decide About Together 10
- Meetings 17
  - Simple Tools for Effective Meetings with Kids 18
  - Meeting 1: Rounds and Agreements 22
  - Meeting 2: How We Decide Together 26
  - Meeting 3: What Are We Going To Do Together 36
  - Meeting 4: Let's Make It Happen 41
  - Meeting 5: Changing It Up 46
  - Meeting 6: Who's Going To Do What 58
  - Meeting 7: Complex Proposals 69
- Cheat Sheets for Facilitators 79
  - Resolving Objections Cheat Sheet 80
  - Selection Process Cheat Sheet 81
  - Proposal Synthesis Cheat Sheet 82
- Appendices 85
  - Appendix 1: Consent Games 86
  - Appendix 2: Round Prompts 89
  - Appendix 3: Example Agreements from Pathfinder 91
  - Appendix 4: Additional Resources 93
- Acknowledgements 96

PART ONE

Introduction

Why sociocracy with children?

Children learn new games all the time, and they delight in tweaking and changing the rules. I see practicing sociocracy as learning the rules of a new game called "Let's Decide Together." Who will do which chores? Where should we go on a trip? How will we handle profanity? What are the rules for screen time? Making these decisions with children can be hard and choices often ultimately fall on the shoulders of adults, creating a power imbalance and possible conflict. Sociocracy offers a set of tools that can help. These tools can be applied anywhere children and adults are empowered to decide together, from families, clubs, cooperatives and schools, to neighborhoods, towns, and even across countries.

I remember vividly when an urgent situation about internet safety came up in the school I founded. Some of the younger children had searched for "butt stuff" and accidentally stumbled upon some… let's say, *very* inappropriate content, despite our firewalls and parental controls. I was terrified that parents would pull their children. As a director, I was tempted to respond reactively with an emergency, top-down decision. It was a perfect test case to see if we could trust our collaborative sociocratic process. Despite the feeling of urgency, we stuck to our agreements and went in rounds with the children, parents, and staff, asking, "What would help you feel safe with children using the internet?" Parents wanted guidelines about how to engage in chat platforms and about safety with strangers on the internet. Kids wanted to be able to watch "normal" YouTube rather than the kids-only version. Staff wanted to be able to ask to look at children's screens to ensure safety agreements were being followed. There were discussions about defining what is appropriate content, with consideration given to topics from pornography to conspiracy videos or violent content. Through the consent decision-making process, a solution arose that met everyone's needs for both safety and freedom. Children agreed to attend a monthly Internet Safety Certification where topics would be explored in depth, and to sign an agreement about how to use the internet. We created it together, after all voices were heard. With this agreement in place, our community was able to move forward together as a team. This is just one of many examples where using sociocracy with children strengthened our community.

Using sociocracy with children, I have seen them grow into their power, swelling with pride as they step into responsibility. I've seen shy children grow into confidence from being truly heard as they learn to speak up with their opinions. I've seen children become accustomed to being treated with respect by adults, children who are comfortable disagreeing with and questioning authority. Teachers have told me they feel relief at not having to know the answers all of the time about how to manage difficulties that come up in class. They are amazed by the innovative solutions that students come up with. Parents have told me stories of their children introducing consent decision-making at home and working out previously insurmountable family disagreements by seeking a middle ground that everyone could live with. A formal study at the Rainbow Community School in Asheville, NC, USA, found that students practicing sociocracy have a much greater ability to adopt the perspectives of others than their peers at conventional schools[1]. Practicing sociocracy with children can truly change lives.

On a larger scale, The Neighborhood Children's Parliaments in India[2] connect thousands of children in a sociocratic network of neighborhood groups, each with child representatives to the state and national levels. These children discuss real problems and consent to steps they can take to address them. Children's parliaments have successfully improved school and public sanitation, lobbied for inclusion of disabled students in schools, founded playgrounds and public libraries, and worked to end sexual trafficking of minors. In one neighborhood parliament circle, children abused by alcoholic fathers came together to make a dramatic presentation to their village about their stories. Through the presentation, they told their stories, raised awareness, and succeeded, with the help of the town councilor, to start a new rehabilitation program and a program against domestic violence. The tools of sociocracy serve to support children's organizing to address their needs. Currently, a Provisional World Children's Parliament[3] is forming to help empower children's voices worldwide.

As you'll discover, sociocracy is a way to share power where everyone's voices are heard and everyone's needs are considered. Not only is using sociocracy with children a valuable teaching tool, but it also creates a deep sense of shared purpose and belonging. I firmly believe that using sociocratic tools with children can help create a more humane world.

---

[1] Renee L. Owen & John A. Buck (2020): Creating the conditions for reflective team practices: examining sociocracy as a self-organizing governance model that promotes transformative learning, Reflective Practice
[2] https://childrenparliament.in/
[3] https://wcp.earth/

What is sociocracy?

Sociocracy is a form of governance and set of decision-making tools that offers effective ways to share power. Using sociocracy, decisions can be more inclusive, egalitarian, and harmonious, therefore better meeting everyone's needs.

Majority rule or consensus, vs sociocracy

In a top-down hierarchy, decisions can be made quickly and it's clear who is in charge. However, people at the "bottom" can be completely left out of decision-making. It's inherently unequal. Many people in families, schools, and organizations are dissatisfied with an authoritarian structure, but it's hard to know what to do instead.

Majority rule decision-making, where decisions are made through a popular vote, is familiar to most people. The advantages of majority rule are that clear decisions can be made quickly and arguments can be heard for both sides. The disadvantages include contentious debate and a disaffected minority who may feel their voices don't matter. It can quickly degrade into a tyranny of the majority.

Consensus considers the voices of all, including the minority, but one person can block a measure from being passed indefinitely because everyone has to be in agreement. This can lead to the tyranny of the minority and very long meetings. As you've probably experienced, something as simple as deciding what to eat for dinner can be drawn out and frustrating when trying to reach consensus.

Consent decision-making in sociocracy includes the voices of the minorities, but differs from consensus in that objections are sought out and harvested to make proposals better. Rather than blocking a decision, objections can help move the process forward. Sociocracy helps by combining the egalitarian values of participatory decision-making along with the clarity that comes from clear roles and decision-making domains, making for the best of both worlds.

About this book

About the author and the origins of this book

I founded Pathfinder Community School, a self-directed learning community for children ages 5-14 in Durham, NC, USA. From the very beginning, the program was designed to use sociocracy with children. Through several years of implementation, we discovered that some of the practices of sociocracy were complicated and cumbersome for children to learn. Keeping the heart of sociocracy (consent, inclusion, and continual improvement through feedback), we streamlined the process and broke it down into small steps that seemed to work better, especially for younger children. Feedback from families using sociocracy at home served to improve this book for family audiences as well. This workbook will help you include children in decision-making in a way that works for both children and adults.

How to use this workbook

This workbook is for anyone who wants to make decisions together with children. The process can work for families, homeschool cooperatives, youth groups, afterschool programs, school clubs, or classrooms. Sociocracy will empower all children involved to work towards shared goals.

This book is meant to be worked through with children making collaborative decisions together in a small group. Adult facilitators will read through the instruction pages for each meeting, then take the agenda script as a jumping-off point for the meetings with children.

Each meeting in this workbook covers a different topic in sociocracy and the meetings build on each other. The meetings are offered as useful tools; take what works for you and leave the rest. It will be helpful to read all of the meetings, even if you only adopt parts of the process, as the concepts reinforce and build on each other. Families might find it easier to combine some meetings, as more topics can be covered in one sitting with just a few children. Schools and larger groups will find working through the meetings in progression and the additional worksheets to be most helpful.

These tools are simplified for working with children. Sociocracy also includes more complicated structures, not covered in this book, for use in communities larger than a single family or classroom. Double-linked circles are one such structure enabling sociocracy to work on a school-wide basis, or with hundreds of children participating in smaller interconnected circles.

The Children's Parliaments in India is a great example, connecting many thousands of children using sociocracy[4].

> **NOTE**
> Circle structures in schools will not be covered in this book, but are available in an online free resource as an addendum:
> https://sociocracyforall.org/lets-decide-together-2021

More resources for learning about sociocracy in-depth are listed in Appendix 4: Additional Resources (page 93).

Notes on age range

This book is intended for use with children ages 5-12. The meetings are meant to be fun! For ages 13 and up, you could modify the material slightly and cover two or more topics per meeting rather than one. For older teens, materials intended for adults may be perfectly adequate. However, remember that teens (and adults!) still enjoy connecting and playing games.

What works for different age groups

5-7 year olds	• Meetings 1-5
8-10 year olds	• *All of the above* • Meeting 6
11+ year olds	• *All of the above* • Meeting 7

---

[4] https://www.powertothechildren-film.com/ — Power to the Children, a documentary about the Children's Parliaments in India.

Common questions

What is the cultural context needed for sociocracy to be implemented successfully?

A collaborative and compassionate culture is necessary to implement sociocracy successfully. Children must feel that they are safe, seen, and heard. Complementary methods to sociocracy include Nonviolent Communication (NVC) and Restorative Practices, which are conflict resolution and relationship-building tools. It's important in both families and larger groups of children to have a conflict resolution process that is clear and consented to. NVC and Restorative Practices provide support for these important conversations. See Rounds for Conflict Resolution (page 90) for an example process that works.

Perhaps the most important aspect for success is an attitude of leaning into making mistakes, being willing to try things out, and being OK with failing. The ability to learn from mistakes is crucial to making sociocracy work in any context.

How does sociocracy integrate with social and emotional learning?

Sociocracy promotes social and emotional learning in several ways. The first is in speaking and listening skills practiced by talking in rounds. Check-in and relationship-building rounds can serve to help people identify how they are feeling and share with others. Identifying group needs and the needs of individuals through the sociocratic process can build empathy and awareness of how others are affected by one's own behavior.

What is needed to implement sociocracy at the school-wide level?

First and foremost, **support from the administration**. If there is a rigid top-down hierarchy at the administrative level, this may not work to create true student empowerment. The domains of the administration and the teachers need to be clear, as well as the domains of the students. Most schools do not operate democratically and it is difficult to implement sociocracy as a single teacher in a classroom, without support from the administration. It is best if there is a clear commitment to sharing power throughout the organization. If you are implementing as a sole teacher, make sure that you have the power within your classroom to hand over a specific domain to the children. Examples are arranging items in the classroom, how to work on group projects together, how to keep the classroom tidy, or classroom behavior agreements.

Secondly, **ongoing training for staff**. To implement sociocracy effectively, there need to be enough trained facilitators to keep meetings going. Implementing sociocratic facilitation tools can be counter-intuitive at first, so it takes time and practice to use them effectively.

Lastly, **evaluation and continued consent**. Make sure to consent to using sociocratic tools for a limited term and to check in to evaluate how they are working. Feel free to iterate on these tools and adapt them to your specific circumstances.

How do you implement sociocracy at the neighborhood-wide or national level?

Start small, then grow from there! There is a book called *Hello, Neighbourocracy*[5] by the founder of the Children's Parliament movement, which covers in detail how to start and support a neighborhood children's parliament. You can also reach out to and support the World Children's Parliament[6] and Indian Neighborhood Children's Parliament[7].

---

[5] https://www.leanpub.com/helloneighbourocracy/
[6] https://wcp.earth/
[7] https://childrenparliament.in/

What will you decide about together?

Children's domain

In our world, it is normal for adults to hold all the power by default. It is important when using this book to give children real power and responsibility. At the same time, not everything is appropriate for children to decide about. What is a safe topic for them to decide about? What can you hand over to them completely? As a parent, maybe you can hand over "making lunch on Wednesdays," or "how to spend $20 as a family," or "where to go this Saturday." As a teacher, maybe you can hand over what activities children have available during free time. One use of sociocracy is to modify practices, such as how to keep common areas tidy, or agreements about how everyone wants to be treated. In sociocracy, areas of responsibility and decision-making power are called **domains**.

Domain examples:

- A room in a house
- Common areas in a school or house
- A weekly meal
- School clubs
- Specific projects
- A discretionary budget
- Improvements to your community

Be aware of what domains you want to keep for yourself and when you want a consent vote. Within communities using sociocracy with children, there are a broad range of decisions given over to the children. At Pathfinder, the school I founded, we reserved health and safety decisions for the adults. A mistake I've learned to avoid is giving the children power and then taking it away, for example by letting children decide where to go on a field trip, then going somewhere completely different without asking.

It's important to know if there are limitations on decision-making imposed from the existing power structures, for example in a school that uses an authoritarian hierarchy at the administrative level, or concerns about liability or other legal issues. Check to make sure that the children's domains will not be undermined by decisions from above. I once heard a story from a school where the principal undermined a student budgetary decision by taking the budget away after the students had decided on it, which was very disheartening. This kind of inconsistency erodes trust and undermines the process.

At Pathfinder, we used sociocracy to decide the school rules, how to spend a discretionary children's budget, what classes and workshops were offered, and where to go on field trips.

Bonus: giving children a set amount of money and letting them decide how to spend it is a worthwhile math, budgeting, and collaboration exercise all in one.

Whatever domain the children have control over, give it to them completely. It's important to not overstep the boundaries of the children's domain by inserting your opinions or making decisions for them, as tempting as that can be. The resulting empowerment will be worth the loss of control you may experience. I remember being scared to let the children at Pathfinder decide rules about hot topics like screen time and profanity, but they rose to the occasion and it was a beautiful process. Lean into it and remember that you're helping children grow by letting go and letting them decide for themselves. To ensure power-sharing, it's best to train a youth facilitator as soon as the processes have been modeled sufficiently and to let the children participate in the proposal-making process as much as possible. At the same time, make sure to first model facilitation and proposal-making long enough for the children to learn from you.

Aims of the group

Aims describe the activities that bring the group together and the kinds of decisions that will be made within a domain. Be transparent that one aim of the group is to learn and practice sociocracy together using this workbook. Together you will work on other aims in more depth with the children in Meeting 3: What Are We Going To Do Together (page 36).

Here are a few examples to help you get started brainstorming:

Sample domain	Sample aims
A room or common area in a school or house	• Keeping the area tidy • Deciding how to use the area • Decorating the area
A weekly meal	• Meal planning • Budgeting and shopping for the meal • Cooking the meal
School clubs	• Choosing how to do the club activity • Practicing democratic governance • Purchasing items for the club
Specific projects	• Deciding which project to do (ex: the topic of a school project, the kind of craft project, etc)
A discretionary budget or shared allowance	• Spending the budget • Using the purchased items
Improvements to your community	• Coming up with solutions to address problems • Implementing changes

Examples of consent decision-making in context

Consent decision-making can help with daily decisions that come up at schools, afterschool programs, camps, or at home, such as "How shall we divide up chores?" and "What shall we eat for lunch?" However, contexts differ and so do the problems in each context. The examples in this book are aimed to be as broad as possible. Hopefully, the following real-life examples will give you an idea of what kinds of decisions can be made by children in specific contexts.

Deciding at home

- What playground to go to
- How to spend a weekend day, including who needs to get rides where and when
- What movie or TV show to watch, including when to pause, whether or not to change movies when someone is scared, etc
- What allowance kids should get
- How to divide Halloween or piñata candy between siblings
- How to determine who is in which bedroom when moving into a new house
- How to store toys in a shared space
- What to eat for a shared meal while considering different diets and preferences, ex: veganism, paleo, gluten free, just plain picky eaters
- How to organize the kitchen

Most of these decisions were made with Meeting 4: Let's Make It Happen (page 41).

Deciding at summer camp

- How to spend $50 (ex: shovels for digging, seeds to plant, a kiddie pool)
- What activities to do each day (ex: art, playing games, turning on the sprinkler in the yard)
- Where to go on field trips (ex: a museum, a local river)

Deciding at school

- Event planning such as the prom, talent shows, end of year parties, and festivals
- Fundraising activities such as selling donuts or running a lemonade stand
- Running a school cafeteria once a week including meal planning, budgeting, cooking, working the register, and waiting tables
- What movie to watch in a movie club
- What to spend discretionary funds on (ex: in participatory budgeting exercises). Examples of purchases:
  - Foam swords

- Cushions for pillow forts
- Field trip funding
- Gymnastic mats
- Art supplies
- Science equipment
- Toys and games
- Playground equipment
- Laptop computers
- Lab equipment
- A membership at a shared sports facility
- Food and decorations for a school dance

I have also seen students bring up proposals to the wider school community, including:

- **Changing the school schedule.** At Morey Flextech High School, there used to be only 3 minute breaks between classes. The students successfully lobbied for longer breaks and the decision was consented to by the whole school.
- **Changing the rules of the school.** At Pathfinder, we had weekly meetings to change the rules using Meeting 5: Changing It Up (page 46). The students decided to change the rules about things like the noise levels, the purpose of specific rooms, how to take care of shared resources, and where to go on field trips.
- **Adding to the school facilities.** At Rainbow Community School in North Carolina, some students wanted a wooden stage for their dance performance. The school administration countered that there was a very limited budget. The students came up with a proposal to get materials and labor donated to build a new stage at low cost, and they danced in a recital on the stage in the same year.

Deciding in a neighborhood

- Problem-solving community needs such as:
  - Sanitation
  - Health care
  - Education
  - Infrastructure
- Direct action to solve problems such as:
  - Founding a library
  - Building a playground
  - Planting trees
  - Organizing community events to build awareness around issues

- Advocating for change at the local and national level such as:
  - Petitioning for alcohol shops to be closed
  - Asking for street lights to be replaced
  - Advocating for children with disabilities to be included in the education system

Decision-making vs doing stuff together

The meetings in this book fall under the umbrella of decision-making meetings to decide how you do things together as a group. I highly recommend alternating each decision-making meeting with a time where you get together and actually do stuff. If it's a baking group, try out recipes. If it's an art club, make some art. If it's a political action group, reach out to representatives or protest. It's important to remember that the purpose of making decisions together is to organize how you accomplish the goals of the group. After you do stuff together, you can use these meetings to evaluate how things are going, make changes, and keep going with continuous improvement through feedback.

PART TWO

Meetings

Throughout the rest of the book, we'll introduce meetings to help you make decisions together with children using sociocratic processes. We start out with tips to help you have successful meetings in general, then walk through the individual meetings. Each meeting contains preparation, examples, and an agenda to be read aloud. Some meetings also contain optional worksheets. It's recommended to work through these meetings in the order presented, as they introduce skills and processes that build on each other.

Other resources are also provided later in the book, including Cheat Sheets for Facilitators (page 79) and the Appendices (page 85).

Simple tools for effective meetings with kids

Group size

This process will work best with a group of fewer than 15 children. In a larger group such as a school class, it may be useful to take turns meeting with children in groups sized 15 or fewer. Meetings can be run with 30 children, but younger children may quickly get worn out.

Honor the meeting timer!

When you're meeting with children, the shorter, the better. I recommend starting with 15-minute timers and seeing how it goes from there, adjusting for the attention spans of various groups. Be careful to limit the time of the meetings to 30 minutes or less, if possible, even with older children. Never go over the time limit without getting consent for extending the meeting. Don't be afraid to politely interrupt whoever's talking, for example, "Before you finish your thought, I noticed the timer just went off and want to get a quick consent for extending the meeting for two minutes so you can finish." You might extend the meeting by a few minutes (with a new timer!) to wrap up an important topic, or to let someone finish a thought. However, it is essential in all meetings to consent to the duration, set a timer, and never ignore it. Honoring everyone's time builds a sense of safety around group agreements and boundaries.

One topic per meeting

With children, we found one topic per meeting to be most effective. Children gravitate towards topics that are important to them, so make sure to be responsive to children's feedback when setting agendas for meetings. Once the group is established, child facilitators and leaders can set the agenda collaboratively with the group (these roles work best for ages 11+).

Talking objects

I recommend you always use a talking object in circles. It's both a reminder of who is talking and who is listening, as well as something that can add a sense of ritual and fun. We've used everything from found objects like flowers, feathers, and turtle shells, to silly toys that are fun to play with. One of the most fun and effective meetings I can recall was done with a "talking toilet" from a playhouse. Each kid said "flush" to indicate when they were done!

I've found that having a special talking object that is beautiful and used only in circles imbues the object with a sense of power and ritual that can help set the tone for meetings, especially when there is deep emotional sharing.

Manipulatives

Many people listen better when they have something to do with their hands. I like to knit at meetings or being the note-taker. You might want to try putting out coloring paper or modeling clay for children to use during a meeting. Showing what you've made at the end of the meeting can be a fun way to connect.

Avoid fidget spinners, handheld video games, anything resembling a ball that might tempt children to throw it, or anything that makes noise. These can be distractions rather than helping children to focus.

Movement and mindfulness

Starting a meeting with a quick stretch can help everyone get their energy out and get ready to focus. I know of a design firm where brainstorming meetings traditionally begin with jumping jacks. With children, we often move like each person's favorite animal or even play a quick round of charades to help with engagement and movement breaks. Another technique that can work to encourage mindfulness is taking a timed moment of silence or three deep breaths together.

Dealing with interruptions and long-winded answers

Is someone taking too long when it's their turn? In the next round, start the round yourself and give an example of the kind of answer you're looking for in terms of length and topic. The group will often take the lead from the first person who talks. You can also limit each person to one idea in a brainstorming session to leave ideas for other people.

In case of interruptions, gently remind the group that the person with the talking object is the only one speaking. Everyone else's job is to silently listen and pay attention.

Feedback, feedback, feedback!

When in doubt about how to proceed on a given topic, ask for feedback from the children. Ask questions such as, "What are the problems you're seeing right now? What new things would you like to try?" or even "How can we be a kinder community together?" You can harvest the wisdom of the group at any time.

Gratitude, celebration, and fun

It's important to focus on the positive aspects of being in a group, as well as on accomplishing goals together. We have a tradition at Pathfinder of starting our weekly meeting with everyone sharing what is going well, or something they are grateful for. We save the statements of gratitude on a poster that everyone can see. In addition, we end every consent decision with a celebration: "Yay! We made a decision!"

Learning sociocracy together can be fun. See Appendix 1: Consent Games (page 86) for example scenarios that you can work through as a group in a playful way to practice consent decision-making. There's also a board game to learn sociocracy together with children called *Keep The Balance*[8] that will be released in 2022 in English from the Sociocratic Center in Austria.

---

[8] https://keepthebalance.games/

Common mistakes

- **Assuming the children will want to take part in every decision you want to make.** In practice, children want to help decide about the things they care most about. To solve this problem, make some meetings optional and topic-driven.
- **Not making sure the adults' and children's domains make sense.** It is much more important to be clear about who decides what, rather than to include children in every single decision. Sometimes after asking the children their opinion, they will want you to make the decision. This is OK! Make sure to get their feedback and consent to letting you make the decision.
- **Assuming the children will proactively engage in the process without support.** Make it as easy as possible for children to make proposals. Gather feedback all the time, by asking questions about what they want to do, buy, or see happen within the domain you're deciding about. Synthesize proposals for them so they have examples of how the process works. It takes time to build trust that you will actually listen to them. It's very important to follow up with the action as soon as possible after a decision is made to build this trust. For example, if purchasing an item has been approved by the group, buy it as soon as possible.
- **Taking power away after having given it to them.** There is nothing as destructive to trust as taking power away from the children. It's important to be clear about domains from the very beginning.
- **Leading meetings that are too long and boring.** Meeting content should be to the point and generated by the children whenever possible, responding directly to their needs and wishes. If you need to shorten meetings, you can eliminate opening and closing rounds or talk about an agenda item over two meetings if the first meeting goes past the timer. Deciding together how long meetings can be is one of the most important decisions to make together.
- **Teaching by talking rather than by doing.** Practicing together is the best way to learn. Use the consent decision-making games in Appendix 1: Consent Games (page 86) to practice in a fun way.

Meeting 1: Rounds and agreements

Clarity of domain

You will need to arrive at this meeting with clarity on the domain the children have power over. See Children's Domain (page 10) in the introduction for information on forming a domain. It is vital that you stick to the domain for the remainder of your time together so that children have trust in the process and know they have real decision-making power.

Rounds with children

Rounds are the discussion format in sociocratic meetings. A round is simply taking turns in a circle to speak. It is deeply effective for teaching listening skills and empathy, strengthening relationships, and tapping into group wisdom. Rounds have an advantage over raised hands in that you hear from everyone and not just those who are the most outspoken.

You could do an infinite number of meetings just focused on talking in rounds. The appendix includes ideas for round prompts, including Rounds for Connection and Fun (page 89), Rounds for Feedback (page 89), Rounds or Meetings for Empathy and Emotional Intelligence (page 89), and Rounds for Conflict Resolution (page 90).

Remember to use a **talking object** for rounds. Choose an object with intention. If you are going to use an object that has significance to native people, such as a feather or decorated talking stick, take the time to research its use and present the background of the practice when you introduce the object.

Making a talking object together as a group project can build a sense of community. Some examples are:

- A smooth stick that children take turns sanding down
- A special rock found by the group
- A natural object such as a turtle shell or bone
- A jar full of sticky notes with written intentions, wishes, etc from each member of the group (which can be added to as new members join)

Group agreements

In founding any group, it is important to have agreements in place about the intentions of how you will treat each other in the group. This creates a sense of safety as well as a touchstone to come back to, when conflicts occur—and they *will* occur! The main agenda item of the first meeting is to make a list of agreements of how everyone wants to be treated and to consent to it. This is essential, because without agreements there is no common ground to come back to when things go wrong.

Example agreements:

- Ask before touching others
- Stop when someone asks you to
- Listen to each other

Something like this may be sufficient for your group. For larger groups, see Appendix 3: Example Agreements from Pathfinder (page 91) for real-life agreements at a school.

Sociocratic meeting format

The format for the meetings will always be the same. For younger groups ages 5-7, you can cut the check-in and closing round and limit the meeting to the main agenda item.

Check-in round	Check-ins are a time to connect as a group. The check-in round is a time to hear how everyone feels as the meeting begins. It can also be an important place for sharing. A general check-in prompt is: How are you doing right now? If you have limited time, I suggest asking each person to share with one word, or to show with their faces how they're feeling.
Meeting time	How much time will the meeting take? I suggest 30 minutes max. Set a timer.
Agenda item	The main content of the meeting.
Closing round	How did the meeting go? What went well? What can you learn to do better next time? If limited for time, do thumbs up (I liked it) / down (there was a problem) / sideways (I have no strong feelings) to see how the meeting went, and only ask those with thumbs down to speak about what could be better.

Meeting preparation

- Bring a talking object to the meeting, or bring materials for making a talking object together.
- Create a poster or some other public document for agreements, with room for the children to sign the document.

NOTE
For printable PDFs of worksheets (bordered pages), visit:
https://sociocracyforall.org/lets-decide-together-2021

Meeting 1 agenda: Rounds and agreements

1. Announce the meeting time
The meeting will be ____ minutes. (Set the timer.)

2. Read introduction
Sociocracy is a set of tools to help us decide together. In this circle, you get to decide how to [*your domain*].

Rounds are a way of talking so that everyone is heard. This practice comes from communities of native people all around the world. People take turns holding the talking object. When you have the object, it is your turn to speak. When someone else has the object, it is your turn to listen.

3. Check-in round
How are you doing today?

4. Fun question round
Let's practice talking in a circle by taking turns answering a fun question. (Choose one below or make up your own.)

- What did you have for breakfast?
- What superpower would you like to have?
- If you could turn into one animal, what would it be?

5. Agreements round
How do you want to be treated in this group? Let's make a list. (Write on a poster during the round.)

6. Check for consent
Does this list of agreements look complete?

- **thumbs up** for "I like it"
- **thumbs sideways** for "I'm OK with it" or "I don't have strong feelings about it"
- **thumbs down** for "objection" or "I see a problem"

7. Sign Agreements

8. Closing Round
How did today's meeting go?

Meeting 2: How we decide together

The principle of consent decision-making is a foundational concept in sociocracy. Fortunately, children often seem to adapt to it more easily than adults!

It's worth taking the time to understand consent thoroughly.

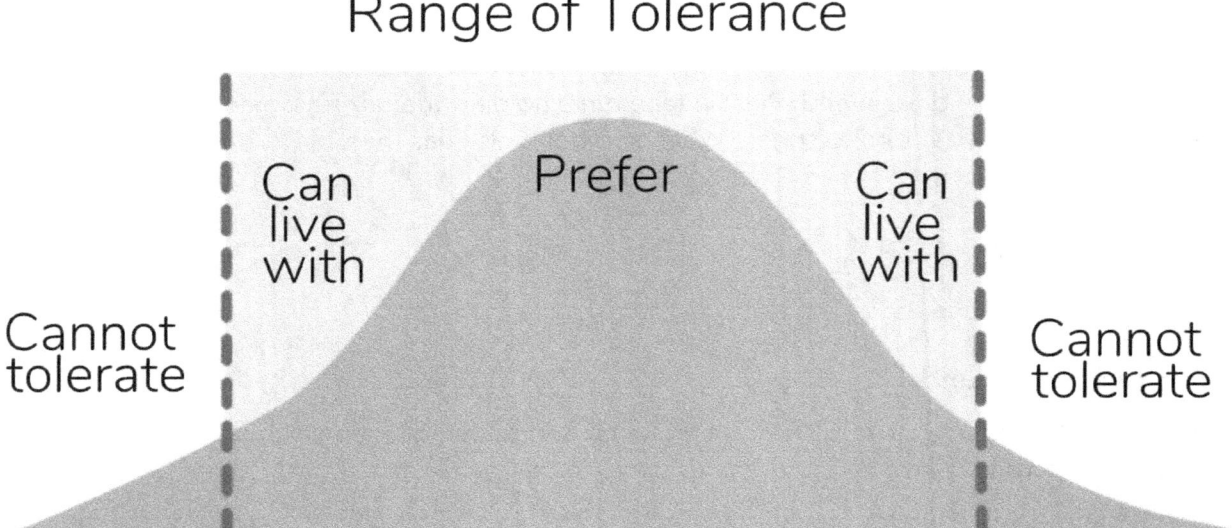

Consent can be thought of as a range of tolerance for an idea. A range of tolerance falls between the lines of what people can live with. What they cannot tolerate would qualify as an objection. Instead of voting yes or no for an idea you agree or disagree with, the aim is to find consent for everyone.

Consent means: I am OK with trying this out, at least for a little while. It's good enough for now and safe enough to try.

Objection means: I see something that's a problem—either *not* good enough for now or *not* safe enough to try.

An objection needs to be backed up with a reason, such as pointing out a danger to making the decision that the group didn't see, or seeing something that will prevent the group from accomplishing its goal.

Consent is not a preference. For example, let's say several people are deciding where to set the thermostat in a room. If everyone voted for their preference, you might get ideas that are all over the place without overlap. If each person considers their range of tolerance, or what they are OK with, consent can be found much more quickly.

Let's say I prefer to have the windows open if it's 80°F out (27°C), while my roommate prefers the temperature to be 73°F (23°C) with the air conditioning on. If we each vote for our preference, we won't find a middle ground. Let's say I can tolerate from 85°F (29°C) down to 77°F (25°C) and they can tolerate from 70°F (24°C) up to 77°F (25°C). There we have a middle ground that we can consent to at 77°F (25°C).

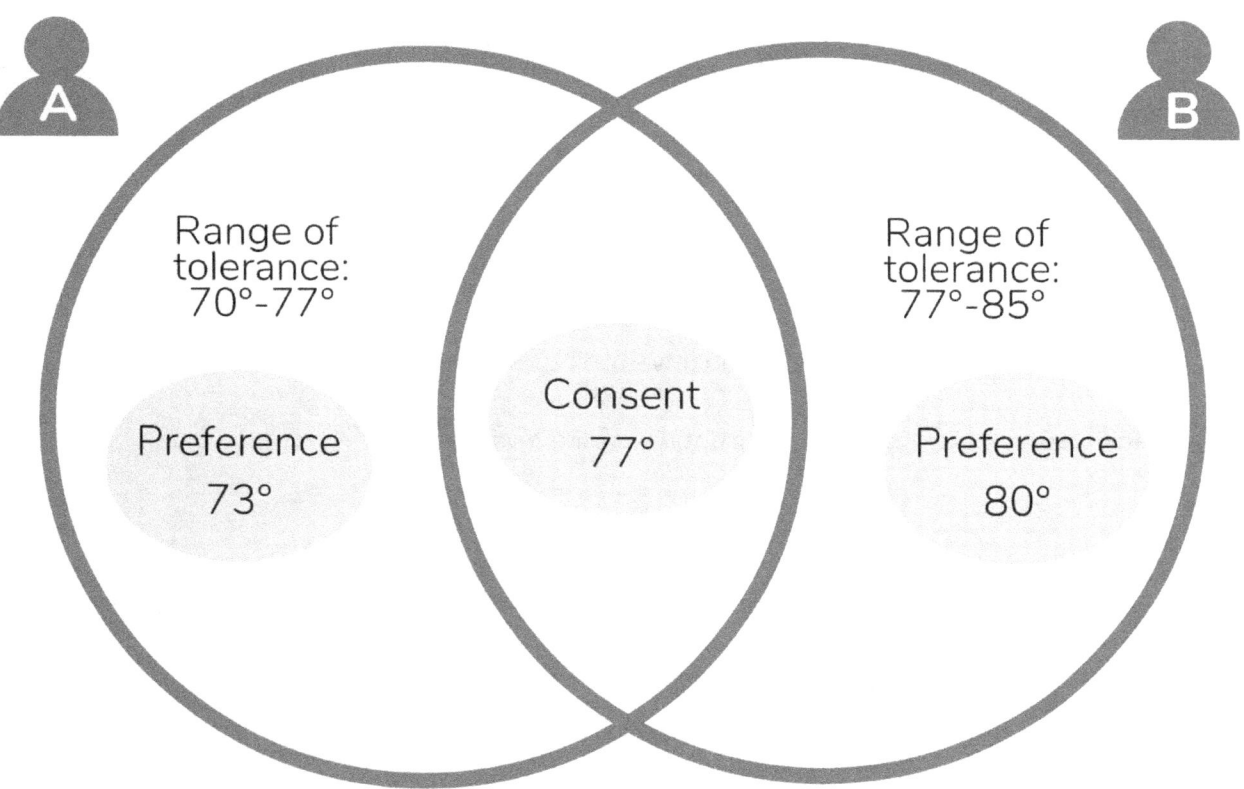

See the Consent & Objections Worksheet (page 35) for help practicing consent.

What to do in case of an objection

An objection is a gift to the group, as it highlights something the group doesn't see. You will likely need to coach children that an objection is not a personal preference. "I don't like it," is not a valid objection unless it is backed up by some reason that the decision goes against the aim of the group, isn't good enough for now, or safe enough to try. Frequently, people are unwilling to use the word "objection" but might share a reaction or concern. Try to resolve the concern the same way you would an objection. It may take some follow-up questions to get clarity on what someone doesn't like about a proposal, and there is usually something valuable there.

Ways to resolve objections include:

Amend

Change the proposal to address the objection or concern.

In today's meeting, you'll be deciding on what game to play that everyone will be OK with. If the objection is that the game won't work for some reason, do a round on ideas for what could make the game work.

For example:

    Facilitator: "It sounds like you're afraid this game won't be fun for everyone. What changes can we make to the rules to make it more fun for you?"

    Child: "It would be more fun if we took turns being 'it'."

    Facilitator: "Okay, can you consent if we take turns being 'it'?"

Concern

Make the concern into a question to ask at the check-in to see, "Is X (concern) happening?"

For example, "What if we check in after one round of the game to see if it was fun?"

Term

Adjust the time before checking in on the decision.

Checking in on decisions quickly and having a set time when they can be reviewed helps people to feel safe trying things out. For example, "Let's try the game for 5 minutes and then stop to check in and see if everyone is OK to continue."

ACT (Amend, Concern, Term)

The acronym ACT and the Resolving Objections Cheat Sheet (page 80) can help you remember how to resolve objections. You may need just one, or all of these strategies, to successfully overcome an objection.

What if you can't overcome an objection?

In practice, I don't think I've ever seen an objection that couldn't be overcome. Validating the person's concern and integrating it into the proposal, whether as an amendment or as a question for evaluation, is very effective. If nothing else works, shorten the term drastically, even to one hour or one day. When asking for consent, ask, "Is it good enough for now? Is it safe enough to try?" or "Are you willing to try this out for X amount of time and then check-in?" Often these questions will help a person find consent.

Hand signs for consent and objections

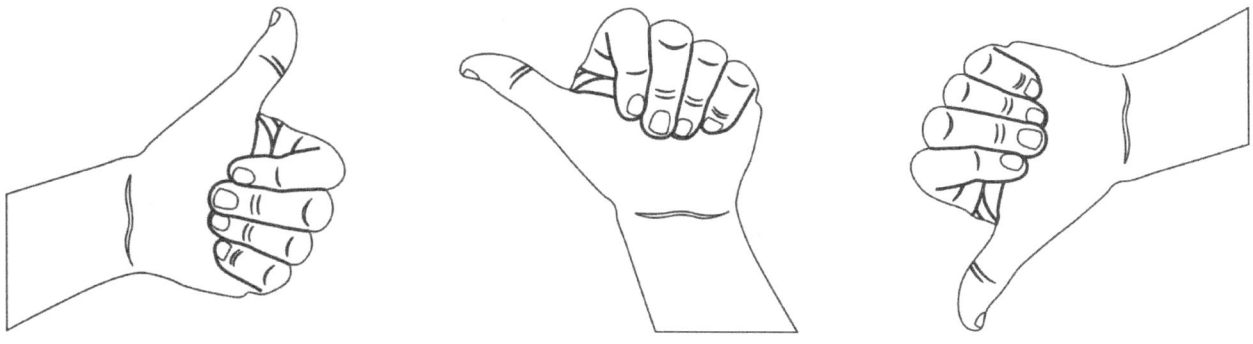

In this book, I use:

- **thumbs up** for "I like it"
- **thumbs sideways** for "I'm OK with it" or "I don't have strong feelings about it"
- **thumbs down** for "objection" or "I see a problem"

An advantage of using hand symbols is that everyone shows what they think at the same time, and so don't influence each other's decisions as much.

Celebrating consent decisions

Once a decision has been consented to, celebrate! A simple, "Yay, we made a decision!" will suffice. It helps to focus on the positive, create group cohesion, and have a little bit of fun.

Sociocratic selection process

Here is the process to use for making a decision between multiple options for what game to play today. See Appendix 1: Consent Games (page 86) for other examples of decisions you could substitute instead of playing a game—for example, what movie to watch, what to eat for dinner, or what to name the group.

The process is:

1. **Read the proposals** (if there are previous proposals)
2. **Nominations and give reasons round**: What game would you like to play, and why?
3. **Change nominations**: Having heard what everyone else has said, would you like to change your mind? (raised hands)
4. **Propose an idea for consent**: The facilitator proposes an idea for consent. Gather and resolve objections.
6. **Celebrate the decision!**

You will guide the children through the process by reading the prompts in the agenda that follows. When proposing an idea for consent, don't simply stick to what the majority of the group has nominated. Think about the reasons given and give a reasoned argument for the proposal you present.

Synthesizing ideas into a proposal and resolving objections are an art form. For more tips, see the Proposal Synthesis Cheat Sheet (page 82). Ideas for fun consent games are also listed in Appendix 1: Consent Games (page 86). They can be a lighthearted way to teach consent decision-making and the selection process.

Transcript of a general selection

In this example, there are no previous proposals, so we generate them in the first step.

Step 1: Nominations and give reasons round

Facilitator: "Let's decide what movie everyone is OK with watching today. We'll start out with a nominations round: what movie or what type of movie are you interested in watching, and why?"

Child 1: "Anything Disney, because it's silly and fun."

Child 2: "Nothing too scary for me."

Child 3: "I'd like to watch How to Train Your Dragon."

Child 4: "I want to watch The Lego Movie."

Step 2: Change nominations

Facilitator: "Does anyone want to change their idea after hearing everyone else? Raise your hand."

Child 1: *(raises hand)* "I like the idea of watching How to Train Your Dragon."

Step 3: Propose an idea for consent

Facilitator: "I nominate How to Train Your Dragon for consent. Thumbs up/down/sideways?"

Child 1: *(thumbs up)*

Child 2: *(thumbs down)* "I don't know if that's a scary movie or not, so I don't think I can say yes to it."

Child 3: *(thumbs up)*

Child 4: *(thumbs sideways)*

Facilitator: "How can we resolve this objection?"

Child 1: "Maybe we can watch the preview and see if it looks scary."

Child 2: "I would be OK if we can pause it if it's scary to me, so I can leave and come back when the scary part is over."

Child 3: "We could look up the rating and see if it's PG."

Child 4: "Pass."

Facilitator: "OK, to resolve that objection, I propose that we look up the movie to make sure it's PG, and if it is, we'll pause the movie if it gets too scary for Child 2. Thumbs up/down/sideways?"

Children: *(thumbs up)*

Step 4: Celebrate the decision

Facilitator: "Yay! We've reached consent! Let's do a little dance!"

Meeting preparation

- Copy the Consent & Objections Worksheet (page 35) if you want to use it with the children.
- Copy the Resolving Objections Cheat Sheet (page 80) and the Selection Process Cheat Sheet (page 81) for yourself if you need them.
- Print out, project, or draw on a whiteboard or poster the weather diagram in Meeting 2 Agenda (page 33), so that everyone can use it as a reference during the meeting.

NOTE
For printable PDFs of worksheets (bordered pages), visit:
https://sociocracyforall.org/lets-decide-together-2021

Meeting 2 agenda: How we decide together

1. Announce the meeting time

The meeting will be ____ minutes. (Set the timer.)

2. Check-in round

How are you doing today?

3. Read introduction

Today, we'll be learning about how we'll make decisions in this group. We'll try out deciding what game to play together, then we'll play it!

In this group, we'll be making decisions with consent. Consent means you are OK with something. It doesn't mean you like it, or it is your favorite idea, just that you are OK with it.

We'll use thumbs up for "I like it," thumbs sideways for "I am OK with it," and thumbs down for "I have an objection." An objection means it's not good enough for now or not safe enough to try.

Let's look one person's consent and objections for the question, "Is the weather OK to go outside today?"

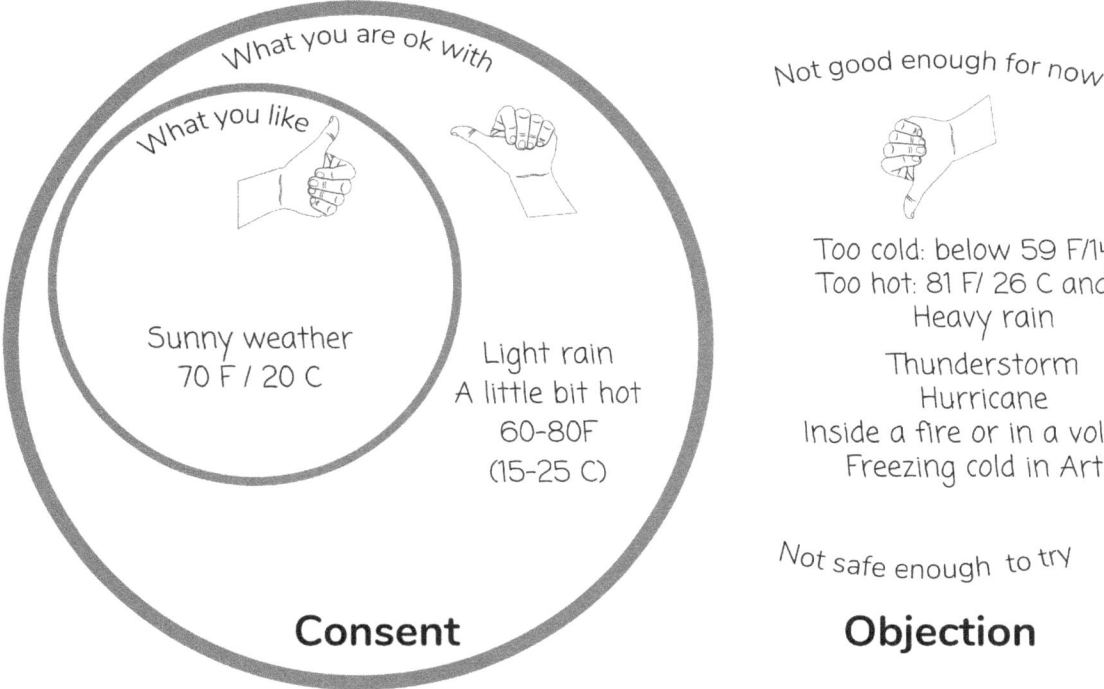

Any way to resolve objections?

Get a jacket or a raincoat
Go hide in a closet (tornado)
Get a fire suit on (volcano)
Wear special clothing (artic)

4. Decide the game

Okay, now it's time for us to decide what game to play today. Everyone will have a turn to say what game they want to play. Then I'll propose one game.

5. Nomination and give reasons round

What game you would like to play, and why?

6. Change round

Did you change your mind based on what others said?

(Ask for raised hands to save time.)

7. Check for consent

I propose we play [*your proposed game*].

Are you OK with trying this game out? Do you have any objections? Remember that thumbs up means "I like it," thumbs sideways means "I'm OK with it," and thumbs down means "I can see a reason it's not good enough for now, or not safe enough to try."

(In case of objections, use the Resolving Objections Cheat Sheet.)

Yay, we reached consent!

8. Play the game!

9. Closing round

How did today's meeting go?

Consent & objections worksheet

Name: _____

Date: _____

Instructions

Pick one of these examples:

- Food
- Movies or TV shows
- Temperature inside
- Temperature outside

Then fill in the diagram below with consent (what you like, what you are OK with) and objections (what is not good enough for now, or not safe enough to try):

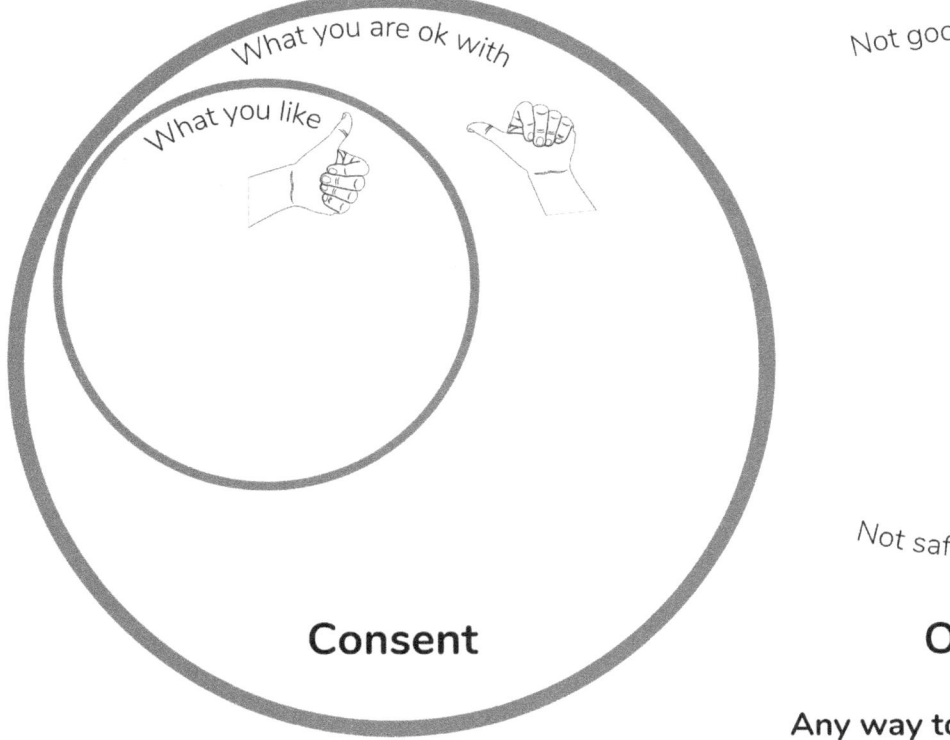

Consent

Objection

Any way to resolve objections?

Meeting 3: What are we going to do together?

Aims describe the activities that bring the group together and the kinds of decisions that will be made within a domain. Make sure the children's domain is clear at this point. See Children's Domain (page 10) and Aims of the Group (page 11) for more details.

With the children, you can say, "You have the power to decide about X" for the domain, and "We will do X together" for aims. You don't have to use the specific vocabulary of "domains" and "aims" with children but this is what they're called formal sociocracy.

Example 1: Shared funds

Your group is raising money and deciding how to use it together.

Domain	Aims
Fundraising and budgeting	• Arranging bake sales and other fundraisers • Deciding how to use the funds

Example 2: Shared resources

Your group is deciding how to use shared resources, such as a room.

Domain	Aims
A shared room	- Keeping the space tidy - Buying new furniture - Decorating the walls - Getting new items for the room

Example 3: Shared responsibilities

Your group is deciding how to divide up household chores.

Domain	Aims
The chores in our house	- Dividing the chores fairly - Making sure the chores get done

Example #4: Shared experience

Your group is deciding what to cook for dinner on Wednesday.

Domain	Aims
What's for dinner on Wednesday	- Choosing a meal that everyone is OK with - Planning the meal - Budgeting for the cost of the meal - Buying the food - Cooking the meal

Choosing aims

In today's meeting, you're going to add to the group's aims of learning sociocracy together and having fun. Hopefully, you'll come up with interesting ideas of what to do together!

In the brainstorming session, the purpose is to come up with more general ideas, but it's fine if kids come up with specific ideas. For example, in the domain of *what's for dinner on Wednesday*, the kids might offer pizza, Chinese food, or soup. All of these fit under the larger, more general aim of *choosing and planning the meal*, which you can synthesize for them and write down. You can take the time to list these ideas to be used in the next meeting as proposals. Write them down on sticky notes and save all the ideas for later, but make it clear you are deciding on the categories of activities today, not the specific activities (that will be next time).

NOTE
With a smaller group or one that moves through the agenda quickly, it's possible to combine meetings 3 and 4.

If you don't have time to do a round or want to leave more time for individual brainstorming, use the Aims Worksheet (page 40) to gather ideas.

You can use the worksheet at a prior time and write the answers students come up with on a whiteboard where they can see them before the meeting. Then you can read through the ideas and come to consent.

The goal of the consent process for this meeting is to answer the question: Is this list complete? One reason to object would be if the list is not complete. Objections to a proposal can also come from the justification that a proposal is outside of the domain, or goes against the aims of the group. For example, with the domain of an *art room*, it would be outside the domain to propose to *paint a mural on the kitchen wall*, because the domain is limited to the art room, so doesn't include the kitchen.

Meeting preparation

- Remember that if time is short, you can use the accompanying Aims Worksheet (page 40) to collect ideas before the meeting and then propose all the ideas for consent as the main agenda item.
- Prepare a whiteboard or other space to collect ideas children come up with.

NOTE
For printable PDFs of worksheets (bordered pages), visit:
https://sociocracyforall.org/lets-decide-together-2021

Meeting 3 agenda: What are we going to do together?

1. Announce the meeting time

The meeting will be ____ minutes. (Set the timer.)

2. Check-in round

How are you doing today? (Alternate question: If your feelings today were the weather, what would they be? Ex: stormy, cloudy, sunny, etc.)

3. Read introduction

Today, we're collecting ideas about what we want to do together in this group. We can decide together about [*your domain*].

4. Feedback round

What kinds of things do you want to do together? (Ex: planning a bake sale, decorating the walls, etc.)

(Write down answers where everyone can see them, like on a whiteboard, poster, or projector.)

5. Check for consent

(Read the answers aloud.)

Do you consent to these actions? Is this list complete? Thumbs up/down/sideways.

(In case of objections, use the Resolving Objections Cheat Sheet.)

6. Feedback round

Do you have any ideas about what we should do specifically? (Ex: if we planned a bake sale, what should we bake? If we decorated the room, how should we decorate it?) We're going to save these ideas for next time.

(Write down ideas for next time.)

7. Closing round

How did today's meeting go?

Aims worksheet

Name: _____

Date: _____

Our domain: _____
  (the area we decide about)

Aims

What kinds of activities do you want to do together as a group?

Activities

What are some specific things you'd like to do?

Meeting 4: Let's make it happen

Before this meeting, gather the ideas from last time on specific activities you could do together. Try to fit each idea on its own sticky note. Now read over these ideas and identify which ones involve budgeting decisions, because I recommend a slightly different process in those cases.

If you're in a classroom, you may want to use the Quick Proposals Worksheet (page 45) for nominating action ideas. This will give students time to think about what they want, before they share in the larger group.

Simple proposals for an activity

Play games, *Go look at bugs*, *Take a walk*, and *Paint a mural* are all activities you might want to do together. Organize them together by how easy it would be to do the activity: how much time and preparation would it take? Explain this so that everyone is clear on what the proposals are and what would be involved.

1. **Nominations and give reasons round**: What activity would you like to do, and why?
2. **Change nominations** (raised hands): Having heard what everyone else has said, would you like to change your mind?
3. **Propose an idea for consent**: Resolve any objections that come up.
4. **Celebrate the decision!**

When proposing an idea for consent, try to nominate something you can do together as soon as possible, then nominate something to work on over time. Having the instant gratification of making a decision and then promptly acting on it will create positive momentum for the group.

When proposing for consent, ask: are these good enough activities to try with the group? Some kids might want to do a majority rules vote for their personal preference, but a majority rules vote leads to people taking sides, creating winners and losers. Instead, just propose one activity and ask, are you OK with trying this out? You can usually choose more than one activity and work something out that meets everyone's needs.

For longer term activities that need more commitment, see Meeting 7: Complex Proposals (page 69). You might want to delegate to a group member or members who are interested in figuring out the details. For example, who will be responsible for doing this activity for the next X amount of time? The facilitator proposes someone for consent.

This meeting is one you will repeat over and over again, as long as the group keeps deciding what to do with the shared time and resources.

Budgeting decisions

Buy a board game, *Buy art supplies*, *Get tickets for a field trip*, and *Buy ingredients to cook dinner* all activities that involve spending money. Making choices about activities involving money need a slightly different process. To help prepare the children to make budgeting decisions, research the costs before meeting with them. If they want to buy a specific board game, how much does it cost? For a field trip, how much would tickets cost? If you were purchasing items for a meal, you'd consider the entire list of ingredients as one item. If you want the children to do the math, you can bring the figures to them to add up. Otherwise, just bring the total cost for each proposed item to the meeting.

Read out loud the items and costs to everyone. Explain that the idea is to purchase what would be best for the whole group, not just one person. Then you can ask children to pick their highest priority items in a nominations round. Use the same selection process as Simple Proposals for an Activity (page 41). Propose consent to purchase the item that has the best reasons for fitting the aim of the group, subtract the cost from the total budget for your new limit, then repeat the process. You can check in with the group about how much money they want to spend that day, or if they want to just buy everything on the list, if they can afford it.

If the selection process turns out to take too long with your group, or if they're losing patience during this kind of meeting, you can use a quick sticky note voting system. Put all the sticky note proposals up and give everyone a chance to put a tick mark on their top 3 choices. Nominate the one with the most votes for consent, and go down the list of most wanted items nominating for consent. This workaround isn't strictly sociocratic, but still maintains the principle of consent as there is a chance for objections.

I have also seen schools use ranked-choice voting[9] for making complex budget decisions, especially when a large amount of money is at stake. The resulting proposal from the ranked choice then goes through the complete consent process.

No matter what process you use, it's important to spend the money as soon as possible so the children can see the results of their decisions quickly. This builds trust in the process and a sense of empowerment.

Meeting preparation

- Bring the lists of ideas for activities and what to spend money on, whether on sticky notes from last time or gathered from worksheets.
- Bring the budget total and the estimated costs of items that have been brainstormed. Then track the totals where everyone can see them, such as on a whiteboard, poster, or projector.

NOTE
For printable PDFs of worksheets (bordered pages), visit:
https://sociocracyforall.org/lets-decide-together-2021

---

[9] https://en.wikipedia.org/wiki/Ranked_voting/

Meeting 4 agenda: Let's make it happen

1. Announce the meeting time
The meeting will be ____ minutes. (Set the timer.)

2. Check-in round
Show with your face: how are you doing today?

3. Read introduction
Today, we're going to decide which activities to start with and what to spend money on.

4. Activity nominations round
(Read list of activity ideas from last time.)

Which one of these ideas are you most excited to try, and why?

5. Check for consent
(Propose the idea with the best reasons for consent.)

Are you OK with trying this out? Thumbs up/down/sideways.

(Repeat process as time allows. Save leftover ideas for next time.)

6. Spending nominations round
We have $____ to spend together. We want to spend the money in a way that everyone is OK with.

(Read list of items and how much each would cost.)

Which one of these ideas are you most excited to buy, and why?

7. Check for consent
(Propose the idea with the best reasons for consent.)

Are you OK with purchasing this? Thumbs up/down/sideways.

(Subtract the cost of the item from the total budget. If they want to spend more of the budget, repeat.)

8. Closing round
How did today's meeting go?

Quick proposals worksheet

Name: _____

Date: _____

Our domain: _____
(the area we decide about)

Activities

What's the first activity you'd like to try? Why?

What else would you like to do?

Budget

What do you think we should buy first? Why?

What else would you like to buy?

Meeting 5: Changing it up

Quick proposals to change how things work

A change-up meeting is a powerful tool to solve problems or embrace opportunities. This process can lead to solid and efficient proposals that address both what needs to change as well as why you're making the change. This format is inspired by agile tools from Agile Learning Centers[10] and Sociocracy 3.0[11].

The categories are:

- **What's happening**: either a problem or opportunity
- **Needs**: group and individual needs
- **What we're trying out**: ideas you come up with to address what's happening and what people need
- **Questions**: to help evaluate whether the proposal is solving the problem, or meeting the needs

I like to use one sticky note for each column, though you can stack notes if it doesn't fit on a single note. Sticky notes help keeps things brief and are also easy to move around.

You'll check in on the proposals for *What's happening* a few times and move them forward on the board to the next *Check-in* column. You can check in weekly, monthly, or however often makes sense for your group. If things are going well and the proposals are working, you will eventually graduate them to your Group Agreements.

---

[10] https://agilelearningcenters.org/
[11] https://sociocracy30.org/

Meeting 5: Changing It Up

Change-up meeting process

Step 0: Start with gratitudes

We like to start by asking the group, *what's working well?*, then using raised hands to answer. It's a nice way to start a meeting and helps keep the focus on what's positive before getting into what could be improved. If you like, you can write down everyone's gratitudes.

Step 1: Announce what's happening

What's happening in our group right now? What ideas do you have for new projects? What problems do you see that need solving? I recommend using the Change-Up Worksheet (page 57) before the meeting to gather ideas, then announce them at the meeting.

Step 2: Connect what's happening to the group's needs

The purpose of making changes is to better meet people's needs. Defining the needs gives you a way to evaluate proposals by asking, "Is this need being met?" The idea of needs might be too abstract for children 10 and under, so they might need help identifying the needs. I recommend doing this on your own, either before the meeting or during the meeting.

Listening to children and identifying needs is an art form, as they usually can't identify and communicate the need directly. Here are some real-life examples of needs children have and how children might express an unmet need.

Example of a need	How children might express the unmet need
Connection	"The other kids are leaving me out."
Safety	"I'm scared."
Understanding	"I don't get it."
Using shared resources	"I want a turn."
Fairness	"It's not fair."
Movement/exercise	(running around)
Play	"It's not fun."
Freedom	"There are too many rules."
Challenge	"It's boring."
Self-expression	(coloring on the wall)
Beauty and inspiration	"It's boring."
A clean and safe environment	"It's gross in here."

Remember that children may have a hard time identifying their own needs, so you might have to ask follow-up questions to identify the unmet need behind their complaint or behavior. This is best done one-on-one, outside of a meeting.

I'm sure you can also think of many other needs! If you're struggling with identifying needs, you can find more lists of needs in Nonviolent Communication's resources[12].

Step 3: Pick one issue to work on as a group for 7-10 minutes

What's the problem? How can we solve it? Go in rounds asking these questions and generate a list of ideas for solutions. If there are more than 10 children present or you're discussing multiple issues, it's helpful to separate into breakout groups. In step 4, these groups will each generate their own proposal, addressing a different issue. Breakout groups work best if children are allowed to attend the group discussing the issue they're most concerned about.

If splitting into breakout groups, I also suggest sending a facilitator to help keep each group on task, especially with younger children. Set a timer for ten minutes, then reconvene with the larger group to announce the proposals.

Step 4: Synthesize the proposal

Look over list of ideas for solutions and synthesize a proposal. Combine the ideas of the group and resolve concerns you've heard at the same time. The proposal should fit on a few sticky notes, so be concise. If a proposal exceeds 2 sticky notes, it's probably best to discuss it in a later meeting or split it into multiple proposals. For highly controversial topics, or when the

---

[12] https://www.cnvc.org/training/resource/needs-inventory/

discussion needs more than 10 minutes, also defer them to a later meeting. If the issue is especially complex, you may need to use the process described in Meeting 7: Complex Proposals (page 69).

Tips for synthesizing a proposal:

- Listen carefully to what everyone has to say. If possible, take notes.
- Arrange what has been said into one proposal. Try not to leave out any ideas. Ask the group, "Did I catch everything you said?"
- Answer any questions posed. Just pick an answer that seems reasonable and see if there are any objections during the consent round.
- If concerns come up, try to integrate the concerns into the proposal as if they were objections. Remember that concerns and objections are positive things that lead to a better proposal.

You can bring the Proposal Synthesis Cheat Sheet (page 82) to the meeting to help you synthesize a proposal.

Step 5: Check for consent

Ask for consent to the proposal with thumbs up/down/sideways. If there are objections, refer to the Resolving Objections Cheat Sheet (page 80) to help reach consent. Collect concerns and questions to evaluate the proposals, then put them on a sticky note in the *Questions* column to come back to at the next check-in (step 6). After reaching consent, don't forget to celebrate your decision!

Step 6: Check-in next time

Try out proposals until the next meeting. After your first meeting, you'll check in with previous proposals after gratitudes, before continuing with the rest of the process. A change-up meeting should be run regularly, for example daily, weekly, or monthly. For short-term gatherings, such as a summer camp, daily check-ins might work well. Weekly change-up meetings work really well if you're in a group that gets together to do activities daily, for example in a school or family. For groups that meet less regularly such as a weekly club, give some time in between change-up meetings to actually practice the proposals and see how they work in action.

Use the concerns and questions you gathered in step 5 to evaluate how the proposal is doing in practice. You can also ask, "Is this proposal meeting the need we identified?" Ask for thumbs up/down/sideways for consent to move the proposal to the next *Check-in* column. If someone objects (thumbs down), repeat the change-up process for what's happening now.

Once a proposal has made it through two check-ins with no objections, the proposal can be graduated to an official list of Group Agreements, ideally displayed somewhere everyone can see them, such as a poster in a common area.

Transcript of a change-up meeting

Facilitator: "Welcome to the change-up meeting. Today, we'll be talking about the problem of running inside. What needs are people having related to running inside?"

Child 1: "I'm scared of people running around so fast."

Child 2: "It's too loud!"

Child 3: "I like to zoom around! It's fun."

Facilitator: "It sounds like we need quiet, movement, and safety. Does that catch what you need? Thumbs up/down/sideways?"

Children: *(thumbs up)*

Facilitator: "What ideas do you have for solving this problem?"

Child 1: "We should run slower."

Child 2: "We should run outside."

Child 3: "We can be careful and run inside."

Facilitator: "I propose the new rule that we can only run outside. Thumbs up/down/sideways?"

Child 1: *(thumbs down)*

Child 2: *(thumbs up)*

Child 3: *(thumbs down)*

Facilitator: "What is your objection, Child 1?"

Child 1: "I thought we were supposed to be able to change the rules. It's not fair. I think we should be able to run inside, just not so fast."

Child 3: "I want to run inside too."

Facilitator: "I object to that idea based on safety. I'm afraid people will get hurt. Plus, nobody seems to be able to slow down if they're playing chasing games."

Child 1: "What if we say no chasing games inside? Can we try it for one day and check-in tomorrow to see if people got hurt?"

Facilitator: "I guess I could consent to that for one day. I propose that it's OK to run as long as you're careful, but still no chasing games inside. Thumbs up/down/sideways?"

Children: *(thumbs up)*

Facilitator: "Yay, we made a decision! We'll try this for one day and tomorrow we'll check if it's working by asking everyone: Do you feel safe? Are you getting the movement you need?"

Finished change-up board for this meeting

Below is a real-life example from Pathfinder. Much to the shock of the adults, the children were able to run inside with nobody getting hurt for the entire duration of the program thus far.

What's happening	Needs	What we're trying out	Check-in questions
People are running inside and playing chasing games.	Safety and movement	Try to run carefully inside. We will try this for one day. No chasing games.	Does everyone feel safe? Are you getting the movement you need? Is anyone getting hurt?

Examples of change-up meeting results

What's happening	Needs	What we're trying out	Check-in questions
People are leaving food in their cubbies.	A clean and safe environment (free of bugs and mice!)	Add "Cubby Checker" to chore list, to remind people to remove food.	Are the cubbies clean?

What's happening	Needs	What we're trying out	Check-in questions
Boys are taking their shirts off in the sprinkler. Girls are not allowed to take their shirts off.	Fairness	Everyone must wear shirts in the sprinkler.	Does this feel fair?

What's happening	Needs	What we're trying out	Check-in questions
Dirty dishes are piling up in the sink.	Cleanliness and to use the shared space.	Everyone must wash their own dishes immediately.	Are dishes piling up? Is the sink clean?

When you check in, you'll have an opportunity to move the proposal (*What we're trying out*) to the next *Check-in* column.

For example, the change-up board below has the domain art room, plus the aims of organizing and maintaining equipment and decorating the room. The proposal of being trained in washing paintbrushes has just been consented to. The next week, this proposal can move to the Check-In 1 column if things are going well.

What's happening	Needs	What we're trying out	Check-in questions	Check-in 1	Check-in 2
People are leaving paint on paint brushes.	Everyone needs to be able to use the shared art supplies.	If you want to use paint brushes, you must be trained.	Are the brushes staying clean?		

The change-up board below is for the domain of shared toys. The proposal has moved to Check-In 1 because it was successful for one week.

What's happening	Needs	What we're trying out	Check-in questions	Check-in 1	Check-in 2
Lego projects are getting messed up.	To use shared materials. To have your projects respected.		Are we sharing Legos? Are people's projects respected?	Put Lego projects in boxes. Take them apart every month.	

Next is an example of a kitchen change-up meeting which could be in a home, school, or office. The practice has been checked in on several times and is now integrated into the community culture, so it can move to Group Agreements.

What's happening	Needs	What we're trying out	Check-in questions	Check-in 1	Check-in 2
The table and counters are getting crusty.	A clean and usable shared environment.		Are the tables and counter clean?		Add "wipe down table and counters" to chore list.

You can view a video of a complete change-up meeting at:

https://sociocracyforall.org/lets-decide-together-2021

Meeting preparation

- On a poster, whiteboard, or projector, create a table with the above columns: *What's happening, Needs, What we're trying out, Questions, Check-in 1, and Check-in 2*. See the Change-Up Board Template (page 58) for an example.
- If you have time before the meeting or are in a classroom context, you may want to hand out the Change-Up Worksheet (page 57) to gather ideas in advance. You can turn ideas into sticky notes and consolidate similar ideas. You can also take notes on ideas, problems, and opportunities outside of meetings as things come up in conversation, then bring these notes to the change-up meeting. Remember that you, as an adult, can also present problems and ideas to the group.

NOTE
For printable PDFs of worksheets (bordered pages), visit:
https://sociocracyforall.org/lets-decide-together-2021

Meeting 5 agenda: Changing it up

1. Announce the meeting time
The meeting will be _____ minutes. (Set the timer.)

2. Check-in round
How are you feeling today?

3. Share gratitudes
What's going well in our group? (Raised hands.)

4. Check in on proposals (starting with 2nd meeting)
How are our proposals from last time going? (Ask evaluation questions.)

Thumbs up/down/sideways for each proposal.

(Proposals with no thumbs down move forward to the next column. Thumbs-downed proposals go back into *What's happening*.)

5. Read *What's happening* and *Needs*
(Read aloud the topics for the meeting. Connect them to needs.)

6. Problem-solving round
(In larger groups, break out into groups of 5-10 children.)

(Set the timer. Work on one issue for 10 minutes.)

How can we solve the problem or take the opportunity?

7. Synthesize the proposal
(Synthesize the proposal, then collect questions for evaluation. Try to fit the proposal and questions on a couple sticky notes each.)

8. Check for consent
(Read the proposal.) Thumbs up/down/sideways.

9. Announce the proposals
(If you broke out into groups, join back together.)

[*Your consented proposals*] are the solutions we're going to try out until next time.

10. Closing round
How did today's meeting go?

Change-up worksheet

Name: _____

Date: _____

What's going well?

What would you like to change?

Why do you need this to change?

How could we make this change?

Change-up board

What's happening	Needs	What we're trying out	Check-in questions	Check-in 1	Check-in 2

Meeting 6: Who's going to do what?

In this next meeting, we'll try a different kind of proposal—not for an action or activity—but for someone in the group to take on a new role. For those used to majority rules elections, this is a very different experience. In majority rules elections, the group can divide into factions and experience contentious debate, and as people only self-nominate, the selection pool is small. The minority may feel disaffected by being left out of the outcome and people who'd fit the role well might not nominate themselves. In contrast to this, sociocratic role selections include all voices, and people may be nominated into roles they wouldn't have picked for themselves, but would thrive in. In this process, everyone has a chance to share why they think someone would be good for a role, which leads to positive feelings all around.

It's hard to convey how profoundly different the process can feel to participants. I've heard people use the words "life-changing" and "magical" to describe their experience. They also report a greater sense of belonging in the group and investment in the outcome.

Consent-based sociocratic selections	Majority rules democratic elections
Roles are defined as part of the selection process. Everyone has a chance to give input for the role and qualifications.	Roles are typically defined top-down by people in power, and not in communication with the affected group, leaving out their input.
People nominate each other as well as themselves, leading to diversity in leadership.	People usually only nominate themselves, leading to people accustomed to power being selected.
Everyone is given a turn to speak and make a nomination.	Usually raised hands are used for nominations, so only some speak.
Selections are made openly and aloud.	Elections are usually made by secret ballot.
Selections are made by consent, guaranteeing an outcome that everyone agrees is at least good enough for now and safe enough to try.	Elections are made by the majority, often ignoring the needs of minority groups.
Increases group cohesiveness, as everyone learns more about each other's needs and concerns, working together to address them.	Inherently divisive, resulting in minority groups feeling left out, their voice having made no impact on the outcome.

Role selections work well in long-term projects. However, if you only have a limited time with the children, such as a 1-week summer camp or 4-week after-school program, I don't recommend role selections. This doesn't leave enough time for people really learn their roles.

Role selections are different from volunteering. Volunteering might seem like an easier process, but often the first person to volunteer is chosen. It may be that another person would be at least as qualified, or might benefit from the experience of performing the role, but they wouldn't think to nominate themselves.

The role selection process can be counter-intuitive at first, but people are often surprised at how positive the experience is. Being nominated by someone else shows a deep trust in one's abilities. Children often love the responsibilities they take on and feel validated being chosen by their peers.

Roles children can fill

Here are essential roles children can take on during meetings, though they need to be modeled first:

Meeting roles	Duties	Ages
Leader	<ul><li>Ensures the circle is in alignment with its aims</li><li>Sets the agenda for meetings</li><li>May check in with members between meetings</li></ul>	11+
Facilitator	<ul><li>Facilitates meetings</li></ul>	9+
Scribe	<ul><li>Takes notes at meetings</li><li>Gives notes to leader after meetings</li></ul>	8+
Timekeeper	<ul><li>Sets timer</li><li>Gives 5 minute warnings to facilitator</li></ul>	5+

Adults—maybe even a single adult—may start out filling all these roles. However, it's best to hand them off to children as soon as possible to help them take on more responsibility. Only select one role per person, whenever possible, to increase participation from all circle members, and to distribute power.

Timekeeper is the first role I recommend handing off to children, because it's most easily understood. Next, I suggest you hand off facilitator and scribe. I have seen very successful change-up meetings, in particular, facilitated by children.

The leader role is the hardest to hand off and may end up being an adult long-term. Steering the group is a big responsibility and children usually just want to take on roles without responsibilities outside of meetings. I've seen children and older youth in leadership positions at the Children's Parliaments in India, and also in established schools using sociocracy, where the roles are well-supported by a larger structure.

Roles outside of meetings

You can also select for roles for outside of meetings, such as:

Roles outside of meetings	Duties
Chore checker	<ul><li>Checks that chores are done at the end of the day</li></ul>
Treasurer	<ul><li>Tracks shared budget</li></ul>
Project leader	<ul><li>Leads a project with a defined term</li></ul>

Role selection process

1. **Describe the role**: Define the term and responsibilities of the role before the meeting. A quick description is enough. Use the Role Selection Template (page 68).
2. **Qualifications round**: What qualities does the person who fits this role need to have? Make a list.
3. **Consent to qualifications**: Is this list complete?
4. **Nominations and give reasons round**: Who would you nominate for this role and why?
5. **Change nominations** (raised hands): Having heard what everyone else has said, would anyone like to change their mind?
6. **Propose someone for the role, for consent**: The facilitator proposes an idea for consent. Gather and resolve objections to achieve consent.
7. **Celebrate the decision!**

The person who has been nominated consents last. This is an important point as the person nominated may not initially want to say yes, but may change their mind and step into the position because of the confidence of their peers that they can do the job well.

See the Selection Process Cheat Sheet (page 81) to help guide you through the live role selection process.

Transcript of a role selection process

Facilitator: "Today we'll be selecting for the role of chore checker. The chore checker keeps track of who has completed their chores for the day by checking off on the chore clipboard. The new chore checker will do the job for 2 weeks. What do you think makes a good chore checker?"

Child 1: "They help me with my chores."

Child 2: "They don't rush me."

Child 3: "They are good at telling if a chore is done."

Facilitator: "Does this seem like a good list? Thumbs up/down/sideways?"

Children: *(thumbs up)*

Facilitator: "Write down who you think would be a good chore checker and why. Then we'll share what we wrote down in a round."

Child 1:	"I think I would be good at chore checker, because I'm short and I can see the dirt really well."
Child 2:	"I think Child 3 would be a good chore checker because they did a good job last time and helped me with my chores."
Child 3:	"I think Child 2 should be chore checker because it would give them a chance to try it out. I'm kind of tired of doing it."
Facilitator:	"Having heard what others said, do you change your nomination?"
Child 1:	"I still want to do it."
Child 2:	"I think I could do a good job and would like to try it out. I'll work hard to help people get their chores done and also make sure everything gets clean."
Child 3:	"I still think Child 2 would do a good job."
Facilitator:	"Having heard what everyone has said, I nominate Child 2 for chore checker for the next two weeks, with Child 1 as a backup in case Child 2 is absent. Thumbs up/down/sideways?"
Children:	*(thumbs up)*

Integrating objections

Seek understanding for an objection. Ask the person who is objecting to tell you more about their objection.

An objection can often be resolved with ACT. The most common way to resolve an objection about the role is to shorten the term of the position, until everyone feels it's safe enough to try. Refer to the Resolving Objections Cheat Sheet (page 80) for more support.

For younger children

It's necessary to keep the meeting shorter for younger children (ages 5-7). For them, I would simplify the process to just three steps:

1. Facilitator presents the role and asks for qualifications (raised hands, rather than a round). "What makes a good X?"
2. Each raised hand makes a nomination and explains why.
3. Facilitator proposes a nominee, checking for consent with thumbs up/down/sideways.

For this process, you'll want to skip opening and closing rounds, or have the children check in with one word.

Meeting preparation

- Write up the Timekeeper's responsibilities and term on a poster, whiteboard, or projector.
- Print out copies of the Nomination Slips Template (page 67) and cut them out (if the group has reading and writing skills).

NOTE
For printable PDFs of worksheets (bordered pages), visit:
https://sociocracyforall.org/lets-decide-together-2021

Meeting 6 agenda: Who's going to do what?

1. Announce the meeting time

The meeting will be _____ minutes. (Set the timer.)

2. Check-in round

How are you feeling today?

3. Read introduction

Today, we're going to select a timekeeper to use the timer in a selection process. It's different from an election where the person with the most votes gets elected. We'll be looking for consent, a decision that everyone can live with. Everyone will give reasons for why they think this person would do a good job. You can nominate yourself or someone else.

(Pass out nomination sheets, then read role, duties, and term aloud.)

Role: Timekeeper

Duties: To keep track of time and set the timer during meetings. To tell the facilitator when there are 5 minutes left.

Term: For the next _____ meetings.

4. Qualification collection round

What makes a good timekeeper?

(Write down where everyone can see.)

5. Check for consent to qualifications

(Read list of qualifications.)

Is this list complete? Thumbs up/down/sideways.

6. Nominations round

Write down your nomination silently on your nomination slip.

(Wait for everyone to write down their nominations.)

Who do you nominate, and why?

7. Check for changed nominations

Having heard others, have you changed your mind? (Raised hands.)

8. Check for consent

(Propose person with the best reasons for consent.)

Are we OK with having [*the proposed person*] as timekeeper for _____ meetings? Thumbs up/down/sideways.

9. Celebrate!

We have a timekeeper!

10. Closing round

How did today's meeting go?

Nomination slips template

I nominate:	I nominate:	I nominate:
_____	_____	_____
because:	because:	because:

I nominate:	I nominate:	I nominate:
_____	_____	_____
because:	because:	because:

I nominate:	I nominate:	I nominate:
_____	_____	_____
because:	because:	because:

Role selection template

Write this where everyone can see during a selection process.

1. Describe the role

Title: _____

Term: _____

Duties:

2. Qualifications round

"What makes a good [*role title*]?"

3. Consent to qualifications

"Is this list complete?"

4. Nominations and give reasons round

"I nominate [*person*], because [*reasons*]."

5. Change nominations (raised hands)

"Having heard what everyone else has said, would anyone like to change their mind?"

6. Propose someone for the role, for consent

"I propose we select [*person*] for the role. Thumbs up/down/sideways?"

7. Celebrate the decision!

Meeting 7: Complex proposals

Formal proposals with a lot of details require more than a simple thumbs up/down/sideways for consent. In order to *really* consent, the group must fully understand the proposal, then have an opportunities to provide improvements and give feedback in the form of reactions and objections before the proposal can be implemented.

I have rarely seen this process in practice with children, but it can be a powerful tool. For most situations, quick proposals and change-up meetings are sufficient. The time to use this more complex process is when people have very divided feelings about a topic, or if it's simply too complicated to figure out in one brief meeting. At Pathfinder, we've needed this process only about once per year.

Some real-life examples of decisions I've seen this used for include:

- Deciding how to divide up the bedrooms in a new house
- Deciding the rules of how to use screens and the internet
- Deciding the rules of profanity vs free speech

Step 1: Gather feedback

Once a difficult situation has presented itself, the first step is to gather feedback from everyone involved. Present the problem and ask what ideas everyone has to solve the problem.

Step 2: Synthesize a proposal

Just like with sticky note proposals, you'll want to synthesize a proposal, perhaps using the Complex Proposal Template (page 76). This can happen outside of meetings. For an example of a complete proposal we worked through at Pathfinder, see Example Complex Proposal Process (page 70).

The cheat sheet has more complete steps for synthesizing, but as an overview, you'll:

1. Integrate all ideas
2. Offer answers to any questions raised
3. Resolve concerns

See Proposal Synthesis Cheat Sheet (page 82) for more on arranging proposals. You can present all the ideas, even those that contradict each other. During the objections process, you'll cross off ideas that people object to or don't understand.

Step 3: Propose idea for consent

Read the proposal out loud.

1. **Questions for clarity**: Do you understand the proposal?
    - You can collect all the questions and answer them at once after the round, or you can answer them one at a time until they arise.
    - Keep going until everyone understands the proposal.
2. **Quick reactions**: Briefly, how do you feel about the proposal?
3. **Consent check**: Is it good enough for now and safe enough to try?

Remember you can use the Resolving Objections Cheat Sheet (page 80) if you need help in the moment.

Step 4: Celebrate the decision

Don't forget to celebrate, especially for a complex proposal that takes more time. A simple cheer is enough.

Example complex proposal process

Initial idea

Purchase a TV within the shared budget.

Step 1: Gather feedback

Before forming the proposal, the idea was presented to the group and feedback was gathered. The feedback informed the proposal in terms of needs and ideas for solutions.

Concerns from feedback rounds:

- People will do nothing but watch TV all day.
- The TV will be too loud and the office administrator in the room next door will be unable to get any work done.

Ideas to consider from feedback rounds:

- We have ages 5-14. Anything on TV should be OK for the younger kids to watch.
- How will we choose what to watch?
- Where and when will we watch the movie?

- Will the show or movie cost money? We want to save our shared budget for other stuff.
- We already have laptops and a digital projector we use for open houses.
- Let's try watching one movie instead of ongoing TV shows.

Step 2: Synthesize a proposal

This proposal was formed in a small group of children who had strong opinions about it, plus one adult who facilitated the meeting.

Steps used for synthesizing the example proposal:

1. Integrating all ideas: about the age range, saving money, and using the projector.
2. Offering answers to questions that are raised:
    - Answering "What rating will the movie have? How will we choose what to watch?"
3. Resolving concerns by:
    - Term: Making it a very short term of one day.
    - Concerns: Integrating concerns about loudness and whether people will "just watch TV all day" into the measurement questions and needs sections.

Finished Proposal

Background
What is happening that this proposal is needed? Problem or opportunity. The idea of buying a TV came up during a budget meeting, but some members at Pathfinder do not want a permanent TV. Some do want to watch movies or shows with their friends.

Needs
What needs are the group experiencing regarding this proposal?

- Fun with friends
- Peace and quiet

Term
One day

Proposal
Member's Circle wants to try out a one time Movie Club at Pathfinder for one hour today only and see how it goes. The movie showing will be from 12:30 to 2:30pm in the conference room. The Movie Club will meet after the morning meeting to decide today's movie by a nominations and selection process.

The movie must be:

- PG or G rated
- Free to stream on Amazon Prime or Netflix

The office administrator gets to control the volume. If it is too loud, they can ask the Movie Club to stop the movie. If it goes well today, we might try Movie Club again in the future.

Questions for evaluation
- Is it too loud?
- Did everyone watch a movie instead of doing other stuff?
- Was it fun?

Step 3: Propose idea for consent

Read the proposal out loud.

1. Questions for clarity:

    Facilitator: "Do you understand the proposal?"

    Child: "Um… who gets to decide the volume?"

    Facilitator: "The administrator gets to decide the volume."

    Child: "What if I think it's too loud?"

    Facilitator: "What if we amended the proposal to say anyone can knock on the door and say it's too loud? Would that work for you?"

    Child: *(thumbs up)*

2. Quick reactions:

    Facilitator: "Briefly, how do you feel about the proposal?"

    Child 1: "I like it. I want to watch movies."

    Child 2: "Me too."

    Child 3: "I'm worried people won't do other stuff and everyone will just watch the movie and I won't have anyone to play with."

Facilitator:	"That would be a bummer! What if we check in tomorrow to see if that happens. Is that OK with you?"
Child 3:	"Sure, I guess that's OK."

3. Consent check:

Facilitator:	"Is it good enough for now and safe enough to try?"
Children:	*(thumbs up or sideways)*

Step 4: Celebrate the decision

Facilitator:	"Yay! We did it!"
Children:	"Woohoo!

Meeting preparation

- Gather feedback on the issue, either in a meeting or via the Complex Proposal Worksheet (page 75).
- Formulate a finished proposal to bring to the meeting, using the Complex Proposal Template (page 76).

NOTE
For printable PDFs of worksheets (bordered pages), visit:
https://sociocracyforall.org/lets-decide-together-2021

Meeting 7 agenda: Complex proposals

1. Announce the meeting time
The meeting will be ____ minutes. (Set the timer.)

2. Check-in round
How are you doing today?

3. Read the proposal

4. Clarifying questions round
Do you have any questions about the proposal?
(Write down questions, then answer all at once.)

5. Quick reactions round
What do you think of the proposal?

6. Check for consent
Thumbs up/down/sideways.

7. Closing round
How did today's meeting go?

Complex proposal worksheet

Name: _____

Date: _____

What are your feelings about this problem or opportunity?

What needs does the group have?

What might go wrong?

What do you think we should do next?

Complex proposal template

Title: _____

Background

Why do we need this proposal? What problem or opportunity is there?

Needs

What needs does the group have related to this proposal?

Term: _____

Proposal

Questions for evaluation

PART THREE
Cheat sheets for facilitators

Resolving objections cheat sheet

Amend

Change the proposal to address the objection or concern. For example:

- "It sounds like you have concerns. What can we change to help you feel better?"
- "Let's do a round on how to solve this problem."

Concern

Make the concern into a question to ask at check-in. For example:

- "Is [*the concern*] happening?"
- "Did [*the concern*] cause the problems we feared it might?"

Term

Change the time to check in on the decision. For example, "What if we check in to see how it's going in [*new time frame*]."

Follow up

After offering a solution, ask the person who made the objection, "Does this work for you? Are you OK with moving forward for now?"

Repeat the process until consent is found, then celebrate!

Selection process cheat sheet

1. Read the proposals (unless generating proposals in step 2)

2. Nominations and give reasons round

"What do you choose, and why?"

3. Change nominations (raised hands)

"Having heard what everyone else has said, would anyone like to change their mind?"

4. Propose an idea for consent

"I propose [*idea*]. Thumbs up/down/sideways?"

5. Celebrate the decision!

Proposal synthesis cheat sheet

1. Gather feedback

Listen carefully and take notes.

2. Synthesize a proposal

Synthesize what's been said into one proposal. Try not to leave out any ideas. Ask, "Did I catch everything you said?" Answer any questions posed.

3. Propose idea for consent

Choose an idea that seems reasonable and see if there are any objections. Read the proposal out loud and resolve any objections.

4. Celebrate the decision!

PART FOUR
Appendices

Appendix 1: Consent games

The first list is for things that you might actually want to decide on and do! The second list is fun imaginary scenarios to try out. The goal to measure against is that everyone must be OK with the outcome.

Start with open discussion rounds about the problem or idea. Then, use the selection process:

1. Nominate and give reasons
2. Change ideas round
3. Facilitator nominates for consent

For more details, see the Selection Process Cheat Sheet (page 81).

Real-world scenarios

Let's imagine we're deciding on:

- What movie to watch together
- What to eat for dinner
- What restaurant to go to
- Which playground to go to
- Where to go on a field trip
- What kind of pet to get (for our class, for our family, etc)
- What to name a pet
- Who is going to take care of the pet
- What to name a group team or band
- What to set the thermostat to today
- Whether to go outside in different weather conditions
- What game to play right now
- What group project to do together
- What kind of treat to get
- What flavor of ice cream to share
- How to share the candy pooled together from everyone's trick or treating or a piñata
- What theatrical performance to put on together
- What to plant in your shared garden
- What kind of playground equipment would you like for a shared space
- How to calculate a child's allowance
- The standards of tidiness for common spaces
- How to build a blanket/pillow fort
- How to share time with gaming systems (or other toys)

Imaginary scenarios

Desert island

Your pirate ship went down and you are stranded on a desert island. You have coconut trees, a knife, and matches but no boat. What do you do together to survive the first day and night? The group needs to agree on a plan.

Landslide

There's been a landslide and you are trapped in the room you are currently in for the next day until rescue crews can reach you. Look around at what materials you have. How can your team survive? What are the top five items you will use and how will you use them? Agree on your five items and the ranking of how important they are.

Flood

You're on an island in a flooded river. You have a raft but it only fits two people and is so weak it will fall apart after you cross the river once. You also have some sturdy rope (half as long as the river is wide) and whatever everyone has in their pockets and backpacks right now. How will you get off the island? Agree on a plan.

Dream vacation

Your group has won an all expenses paid trip to anywhere in the world. You must decide somewhere everyone is OK going together or the tickets will go to someone else. Where will you go?

$100 improvements

Your group has $100 to spend on classroom or home improvements. What will you spend the money on?

Theme park design

You are all partners in a theme park design company and you have won a new contract. There can only be three features to the theme park. Come up with a design you can all consent to.

Superpowers

Everyone in your group has the superpower of their choice. What are the rules for using your superpowers with each other?

Appendix 2: Round prompts

Rounds for connection and fun

- What is your favorite movie or show?
- What is your favorite color, and why?
- What food do you look forward to eating the most?
- If you were an animal, what animal would you be?
- If you could fly or turn invisible, which one would you choose?
- If you could have only one superpower, what would it be?
- If you could travel in time, what time would you travel to?
- If you could be a mythical creature, what would you be?
- What is your favorite joke to share? (You'll want to limit it to one per day as jokes can take a long time!)
- What is one of your favorite things to do?
- If you could go anywhere in the world, where would you go?

Rounds for feedback

- What do you like about being part of this group?
- How do you think we could make things even better?
- What kind of activities would you like to do together?
- What would you like to buy with our discretionary budget?
- If we could go on a field trip, where would you go?
- What can we do to make our community more inclusive or kinder?

Rounds or meetings for empathy and emotional intelligence

- What does it look like on the outside when you are mad/sad/happy/afraid/etc?
- What makes you feel mad/sad/happy/afraid/etc?
- If your emotions today were a kind of weather, what would they be?
- If how you feel right now was a certain place in the world, what would it be?
- Hold up your fingers to show how you are feeling this morning (1 means "I'm having a really hard time" and 5 means "I feel really great").
- What do you think makes a good friend?
- Describe a time when you felt mad/sad/happy/afraid/etc?
- What does it feel like when you are left out?
- What does it feel like to be included?

Rounds for conflict resolution

These work in this order for parties in conflict and are inspired by restorative practices.

1. What happened?
2. How do you feel about it?
3. What would make it better as much as possible, right now?
4. What do you want to be different next time? What do you want to request from the other person?
5. Can you agree to this request?

Closing rounds

- Rose, Bud, Thorn: a rose is something you enjoyed today, a bud is something you are looking forward to, and a thorn is something that was challenging.
- In three words, how did today go?
- Show with your face how you feel about today.

For more round prompts, see the book *Circle Forward: Building a Restorative School Community* by Carolyn Boyes-Watson & Kay Pranis.

Appendix 3: Example agreements from Pathfinder

This is an example of a living document from Pathfinder, meaning it continually evolves and changes. Words like "respect" and "appropriate" are continually refined through group discussions and new agreements in change-up meetings, as needed. It can be tempting to do all of this work up front and try to figure everything out as the adult in the room. It's not only unnecessary, but it excludes the children from the process. Remember that it's important to start small with something that's easy to consent to as "good enough for now and safe enough to try", then you can always change it and build on it later.

Respect others

People at Pathfinder have the right to be treated respectfully. I agree to treat others with respect, whether member, volunteer, staff, or parent.

- **Stop when asked to stop**
- **No violence** against others, including with:
  - your words: yelling, name calling, etc
  - your body: pushing, hitting, kicking, etc

Take care of stuff

People at Pathfinder have the right to a clean and safe environment. I agree to protect and maintain the shared space.

- **Take care** of Pathfinder shared property
- **Clean up** after yourself
- **No messing** with other people's stuff
- **Follow room rules and safety rules**

Take care of people

People at Pathfinder have the right to peaceably exist. I agree to behave appropriately so that I don't disrupt others.

- Take care when **running**:
  - No chasing games inside
  - Clear hallways of loud/raucous activity when asked

- Take care when **rough housing**:
    - Rough housing in rumpus room only
    - No throwing stuff (except in rumpus room, and only soft things)
    - No climbing or jumping on furniture
- Take care with **volume**:
    - No yelling inside: use inside voices
    - Use earbuds or headphones when asked
- Take care with **profanity and content**:
    - Behave appropriately for a mixed age environment

Participate

People at Pathfinder have the right to have their voices heard and their needs met. I agree to participate in making, honoring, and enforcing the rules of the community.

- **Participation is mandatory in**:
    - Morning meetings
    - Change-up meetings
    - The Culture Committee (taking turns as a member and when involved in a case)
    - Clean-up time

Help resolve conflicts

People at Pathfinder have the right to peaceably exist. I agree to help solve conflicts when they arise.

Appendix 4: Additional resources

Books

- Boyes-Watson, Carolyn & Pranis, Kay (2015) Circle Forward: Building a Restorative School Community, Living Justice Press — A manual for using restorative practices in schools with lots of conversational prompts in rounds.
- Buck, John & Villness, Sharon (2007) We The People: Consenting to a Deeper Democracy, Sociocracy.info Press — The history of sociocracy and the story of Gerhard Endenberg, a former student of Werkplaats Kindergemeenschap who formalized the Sociocratic Circle Method.
- Endenberg, Gerhard (1998) Sociocracy: The organization of decision-making, Eburon — A translation from the Dutch of the definitive text from the originator of sociocracy.
- John, Edwin M. (2021) Hello, Neighbourocracy!, Neighbourhood Community Network — A manual and history of neighborhood parliaments.
- Joseph, Fiona (2011) BEATRICE The Cadbury Heiress Who Gave Away Her Fortune, Foxwell Press — The story of Kees Boeke and Beatrice Cadbury, who founded the Werkplaats Kindergemeenschap in the Netherlands, a school that sociocracy originated from.
- Rau, Ted J. (2021) Who decides, who decides? How to start a group so everyone has a voice, Sociocracy For All — A small book for using sociocracy with a startup group. Simple and streamlined.
- Rau, Ted. J & Koch-Gonzales, Jerry (2018) Many Voices One Song — Shared power with sociocracy, Sociocracy for All
  A definitive how-to manual for sociocracy.
- Rawlston, Wyatt (1956) The Werkplaats Adventure, out of print but available online at: https://archive.org/details/werkplaats-adventure, accessed June 30, 2021 — The story of the Werkplaats Kindergemeenschap in the 1950s once it was well established. A first-person account.
- Simm, Gina (2019) Heart to Heart: Three Systems for Staying Connected: A Manual for Parents and Teachers, Small Batch Books — A great how-to manual for Nonviolent Communication with children in families and school settings.

Articles

- Renee L. Owen & John A. Buck (2020): Creating the conditions for reflective team practices: examining sociocracy as a self-organizing governance model that promotes transformative learning, Reflective Practice.
- John A. Buck and Gerard Endenberg (2012): The Creative Forces of Self-Organization, Sociocratic Center, Rotterdam, Netherlands. View online at: https://sociocracyconsulting.com/wp-content/uploads/2016/04/CreativeForces-updated2012.pdf

Websites

- https://wonderingschool.org/ — Resources and extensive training and consulting on schools using sociocracy. Includes the wonderful film, School Circles, which is a must-see film for anyone wanting to use sociocracy in schools.
- https://sociocracy30.org/ — Organized by "patterns," this resource can help identify bits and pieces of sociocracy to implement one by one. Our change-up meeting is inspired by the concept of "drivers" from Sociocracy 3.0.
- https://sociocracyforall.org/ — The definitive one-stop source for articles, books, videos, training, and more about sociocracy.
- https://agilelearningcenters.org/ — Change-Up Meeting comes directly from Agile Learning Center tools. In this book we have modified it to include consent decision-making.
- https://cnvc.org/ — Center for Non-Violent Communication. There are very useful feelings and needs inventory lists available for free on the website.
- https://hopewildertraining.com/ — My business website for training and consulting with sociocracy in schools.
- https://www.childrenparliament.in — The official page for neighborhood children's parliaments.
- https://www.facebook.com/worldchildrenparliament/ — Facebook page for the Children's Parliament Global initiative.

Films

- School Circles: Every Voice Matters. Directed by Charlie Shread and Marianne Osorio, Wondering School, 2018 — A documentary providing an in-depth view of schools using sociocracy in the Netherlands by the Wondering School project. View online at: https://schoolcirclesfilm.com/
- Power to the Children. Directed by Anna Kersting. Anna Kersting Filmproduktion, 2020. A documentary about the Children's Parliaments in India. View online at: https://www.powertothechildren-film.com/

Games

- Keep the Balance. Anja Ritter, 2021. A consent decision-making game made by the Sociocracy Center in Austria. View online at: https://keepthebalance.games/

Acknowledgements

To my partner, Chris, thank you for helping me through emotional writing blocks, which were much more difficult than the actual writing process. Thank you for putting my feet to the fire with final revisions and edits, the book is much better as a result of your feedback, as hard as it was for me to hear. Finally, thank you for the typesetting and graphics work! I couldn't have done this without your support.

To my friends, thank you for encouraging me along the way.

To Ted Rau, thank you for asking me to write this book, mentoring and inspiring me through your own writing, and supporting me in every step of the process from writing to typesetting to publication.

To CJ O'Reilly, thank you for providing a sounding board about the big picture view of the book, and helping me improve the structure and content of the book immensely.

To Russell Baldwin, thank you for going over the entire manuscript with a fine toothed comb together. I enjoyed our meetings and the clarity you helped me bring to the book by telling me when things didn't make sense to you. The book is so much better for your thoughtful input.

To Shala Massey, thank you for helping me think through the cover design, and making the process I found intimidating at first to be fun and enjoyable instead.

To Sociocracy For All, thank you for providing me with a home for my work. I've learned so much from participating in SoFA about sociocracy as well as running an organization compassionately and getting things done while deeply respecting the people involved. I appreciate the opportunity to publish to a wider audience, and hopefully to help children all over the world experience sociocracy and participatory decision-making.

www.ingramcontent.com/pod-product-compliance
Lightning Source LLC
Chambersburg PA
CBHW081753100526
44592CB00015B/2417